BASEBALL: RUN, THROW & CATCH

BRYANT LLOYD

The Rourke Press, Inc.
Vero Beach, Florida 32964

PHOTO CREDITS:
All photos © Lynn M. Stone except cover © Rob and Ann Simpson

EDITORIAL SERVICES:
Penworthy Learning Systems

Library of Congress Cataloging-in-Publication Data

Lloyd, Bryant, 1942
    Baseball: run, throw & catch / by Bryant Lloyd.
        p. cm. — (Baseball)
    Includes index
    Summary: Discusses the important baseball skills of catching, throwing, and running, including base stealing and sliding.
    ISBN 1-57103-189-8
    1. Base running (Baseball)—Juvenile literature. 2. Baseball—Defense—Juvenile literature. [1. Base running (Baseball). 2. Baseball—Defense.]
I. Title II. Series: Lloyd, Bryant, 1942-   Baseball.
GV868.L56 1997
796.357'2—dc21   97–17457
                                                                      CIP
                                                                       AC

TABLE OF CONTENTS

Running 5

Running to First Base 6

Leading Off Base 8

The Steal 11

Stealing 12

Sliding 14

Throwing 17

Catching Fly Balls 18

Fielding Ground Balls 20

Glossary 23

Index 24

RUNNING

Players on both the **fielding team** (FEELD ing TEEM) and at-bat team run in a baseball game. Most of the running, though, is by the team at bat. A baseball player must run to first base after hitting a ball. Sooner or later the player may run to second base, third base, and finally home plate.

A runner can take a peek at where the hit ball goes. Mostly, though, a hitter should pay attention to running.

In 1876, eight teams banded together to found the National League. The American League became the second big league in 1901. Today both the National and American Leagues are part of Major League Baseball.

Having hit the ball, a batter leaves home plate and streaks toward first base.

RUNNING TO FIRST BASE

On a ground ball hit to an **infielder** (IN feel der), a runner needs to run directly toward first base. The runner should run straight through the base, he should not slide or leap to the base.

A runner going to first base can over-run the "bag" and not be tagged out as long as he doesn't turn toward second base.

After taking a turn toward third, a base runner trots back to the safety of second base.

If the ball rolls into the **outfield** (OUT feeld), the runner needs to run wide to a point right of first base. Then the runner should cut sharply toward first to be ready to continue to second. This move is called "taking a turn."

LEADING OFF BASE

Players who reach first base can help themselves reach second. When the pitcher prepares to pitch to the batter, the runner can leave first and move a few steps toward second. That is called taking a **lead** (LEED).

When the batter hits the ball, the runner is already a few feet closer to second base. The risk, however, is that the pitcher—or catcher— will throw the ball to the first baseman before the ball is hit.

A runner leads off third base as the coach watches.

THE STEAL

If the fielder tags a runner before the runner is back on base, that runner is out. Instead of just taking a lead, a runner may race for the next base as the pitcher pitches. That's called a **steal** (STEEL).

If the batter doesn't hit the pitch, the catcher throws the ball to an infielder at second base. To prevent a steal, the fielder must catch the throw and tag the runner before the runner reaches the base.

A fielder's choice is a situation in which an infielder can throw to either of two bases and likely get an out. A fielder likes to get the lead runner out if possible. In other words, it is more important to get a runner going from second to third base out than it is to get a runner going from first to second.

The runner carefully watches the pitcher.

STEALING

A runner who plans to steal second base tries to take about a 10-foot (3-meter) lead off first base. The runner must dive back to first base if the pitcher throws to the first baseman. The runner also must be ready to run to second.

Too big a lead can be trouble. The first baseman tags a runner too far from base when the catcher threw the ball to the first baseman.

By peeking at his hit, a runner decides whether to run straight to first base or to a point wide of first so he can turn towards second.

A good stealer watches the pitcher's movements carefully and begins a charge to second base as the pitcher begins to pitch.

Stealing third base is more difficult. The catcher has a shorter throw to third than to second base.

SLIDING

By sliding, a runner can quickly come into a base without overrunning it or having to slow down. Sliding is used when the runner expects the ball to arrive at the base at about the same time he does.

Sliding is a controlled fall. The runner falls backward and slides with a foot extended into the base. Older baseball players sometimes use a hook slide. With a hook slide, the runner slides wide of the bag but touches it with a hand or foot.

A fielder's success is based in part on the player's fielding average. That figure tells what percentage of times the fielder makes a play on a ball without making a mistake, or error. A fielder with a fielding average of .975 makes the right play 975 times out of every 1,000, on average.

This runner's slide into home plate beat the fielder's throw.

14

THROWING

Throwing a baseball takes practice and skill. A baseball should not be gripped too tightly. The ball should be at the fingertips, not jammed into the palm of the hand.

When throwing, the elbow should extend from the body at the shoulder. The arm is cocked with the hand behind, above, and to the side of the head. A right-hander throws to the right of the head.

The throwing motion should be "over the top," like a ferris wheel, not like a merry-go-round.

A baseball is usually thrown overhand. A right-handed thrower steps forward with the left foot and whips the right arm behind the head in a forward—overhand—motion.

17

CATCHING FLY BALLS

A ball hit in the air is a fly ball. One of a fielder's jobs is to judge where a fly ball will come down and be there to catch it.

If possible, a fielder should catch with two hands. The throwing hand helps the catch by making sure that the ball doesn't pop from the glove.

Glove open, two hands at work, a right fielder catches a fly ball.

Running toward the ball for a catch puts a fielder in position to step forward and throw.

The fielder holds the glove facing outward for balls hit above the waist. The glove is held open, like a basket, for fly balls below the fielder's waist.

An outfielder tries to catch by running toward the ball. Then the fielder is in position to step forward quickly and throw.

FIELDING GROUND BALLS

A good fielder is always alert. A fielder plays from a crouch with glove open and low to the ground. A ball hit on the ground can't go through, or under, a glove that's held low.

Skilled fielders think of their gloves as buckets. They let a glove swallow up the ball, like a bucket would swallow up water.

The glove is a trap, too. It will open and close. A fielder opens the glove when a ball is hit and closes the glove when the ball goes into it.

You can figure your fielding average or someone else's. Take the total number of chances without error and divide them by the total number of chances.

A shortstop, moving to his left, scoops up a ground ball near second base.

GLOSSARY

fielding team (FEELD ing TEEM) — the team on the defense on the baseball field

infielder (IN feel der) — any of the six players in the infield positions, especially the first baseman, second baseman, third baseman, and shortstop

lead (LEED) — the steps that a base runner takes from a base before the pitcher pitches

outfield (OUT feeld) — the part of a baseball field farthest from home plate; the area beyond the diamond or infield

steal (STEEL) — taking a base during a pitcher's windup and pitch; taking a base during or between pitches without a hit ball

First base won, a Little League runner rounds the bag and turns toward second, 60 feet (18 meters) away.

INDEX

base   11, 14

(base) ball   5, 6, 8, 11, 14, 17, 18, 20

batter   8, 11

catcher   8, 11, 13

fielders   11, 18, 20

first base   5, 6, 8, 12

first baseman   8, 12

fly ball   18

glove   18, 20

ground ball   6

hand   14, 17, 18

home plate   5

infielder   6, 11

lead   8, 11, 12

outfield   7

outfielder   19

pitch   11

pitcher   8, 11, 12

player, baseball   5, 8

runner   5, 6, 8, 11, 12, 14

running   5

second base   5, 7, 8, 11, 12

sliding   14

steal   11

team, at-bat   5

team, fielding   5

third base   5, 13